DRONES
EYES IN THE SKIES

COMMERCIAL DRONES

DANIEL R. FAUST

PowerKiDS
press™

New York

Published in 2016 by The Rosen Publishing Group, Inc.
29 East 21st Street, New York, NY 10010

First Edition

Editor: Sarah Machajewski
Book Design: Reann Nye

Photo Credits: Cover Andreas Rentz/Getty Images News/Getty Images; pp. 5, 27 Bloomberg/ Getty Images; p. 6 https://commons.wikimedia.org/wiki/File-Tadiran-Mastiff-III-hatzerim-1.jpg; p. 7 Ahturner/Shutterstock.com; p. 9 Thatsaphon Saengnarongrat/Shutterstock.com; p. 11 https:// commons.wikimedia.org/wiki/File-Black_Hornet_Nano_Helicopter_UAV.jpg; p. 13 (background) mexrix/Shutterstock.com; p. 14 ERNESTO BENAVIDES/AFP/Getty Images; p. 15 https:// commons.wikimedia.org/wiki/File-CBP_unmanned_aerial_vehicle_control.jpg; p. 17 https:// commons.wikimedia.org/wiki/File-Aeryon_Scout_With_Camera.jpg; p. 18 marekuliasz/ Shutterstock.com; p. 19 Chesky/Shutterstock.com; p. 21 (background) Reinhold Leitner/ Shutterstock.com; pp. 22, 30 gualtiero boffi/Shutterstock.com; p. 23 Bernard Patrick/AP Images; pp. 24, 29 alik/Shutterstock.com; p. 25 dreamnikon/Shutterstock.com.

Cataloging-in-Publication Data

Faust, Daniel R.
Commercial drones / by Daniel R. Faust.
p. cm. — (Drones: eyes in the skies)
Includes index.
ISBN 978-1-5081-4490-8 (pbk.)
ISBN 978-1-4994-1854-5 (6-pack)
ISBN 978-1-5081-4491-5 (library binding)
1. Drone aircraft — Juvenile literature. I. Faust, Daniel R. II. Title.
UG1242.D7 F38 2016
623.74'69—d23

Manufactured in the United States of America

CPSIA Compliance Information: Batch #BW16PK: For Further Information contact Rosen Publishing, New York, New York at 1-800-237-9932

CONTENTS

LOOK! UP IN THE SKY!

Drones have been in the news a lot lately. Do you know what a drone is? "Drone" is the common name for an unmanned aerial **vehicle**, or UAV. It's an aircraft that doesn't carry a human pilot. In the past, drones were radio-controlled aircraft. Today, more and more drones are equipped with **autonomous** control. Drones are becoming more popular as people discover new uses for these flying machines.

International law recognizes two types of drones. Remotely piloted drones, such as the kind you might buy online, fall under your town or city's rules. Autonomous drones aren't currently regulated due to legal issues. Why? It comes down to one question: Who's responsible for the actions of an aircraft that controls itself?

A shoe store in Japan developed a drone to get shoes from high shelves. Customers used an iPad to select the pair they wanted, and the drone found it for them.

FROM SOLDIERS TO CIVILIANS

The first drones were used by the military. These unmanned aircraft were seen as a way to gather **intelligence** without the risk of a pilot being shot down over enemy territory. As **technology** improved, drones became lighter and more advanced. Today, roughly one-third of the aircraft used by the United States Air Force are drones. Drones are also employed by law enforcement and intelligence agencies, such as the Central Intelligence Agency (CIA). More than 50 countries around the world use drones, too.

ISRAELI TADIRAN MASTIFF

CIVILIAN DRONE

The same technological advances that improved military drones allowed drones to make the jump from military to **civilian** applications. As parts needed to build drones became smaller, lighter, and cheaper, drones became something that ordinary citizens could afford. Some drone pieces can even be produced using a 3D printer.

First used in 1973, the Israeli Tadiran Mastiff was equipped with real-time video streaming. It's considered the first modern battlefield UAV.

RECREATIONAL DRONES VS. COMMERCIAL DRONES

Even though drone use among civilians and civilian organizations is on the rise, there are some important points to consider. It's important to understand the difference between recreational drones and commercial drones.

A recreational drone is any drone bought and flown for fun and enjoyment. Recreational drones are a lot like radio-controlled airplanes. There are certain general safety tips that apply to flying recreational drones, but for the most part, anyone can buy a drone and fly it.

RECREATIONAL DRONE SAFETY TIPS

DO

- Fly your drone for personal enjoyment.
- Take lessons and learn to fly your drone safely.
- Contact an airport when flying within 5 miles (8 km) of it.

DON'T

- Fly near manned aircraft.
- Fly your drone higher than 400 feet (122 m).
- Ignore local safety guidelines.
- Use your drone for commercial purposes without permission.

If one day you decide you want to use your drone to take photographs or videos and sell them to a local newspaper or television station, you would then be operating a commercial drone. You need official permission from the government in order to operate a commercial drone.

You don't need special permission to fly a recreational drone. As long as you follow a few simple rules, anyone can do it!

PARTS OF A DRONE

Drones come in many different shapes and sizes. Many military drones are built to resemble aircraft you might be familiar with, such as jet planes. Civilian drones are based on a quadcopter design. A quadcopter is an aircraft that has four **rotors**. Some drones, such as the RQ-4 Global Hawk, are quite large. Their wingspan, or measurement from the tip of one wing to the other, can be more than 100 feet (30.5 m). Other drones are small enough to fit in your hand.

Whatever their shape or size, drones require many of the same parts to function. A drone's hull is constructed from lightweight materials. A light body requires less power to take off and stay in the air. Many drones are powered by batteries. Currently, the military is looking into alternative fuel sources, such as solar power or wind energy, to power drones.

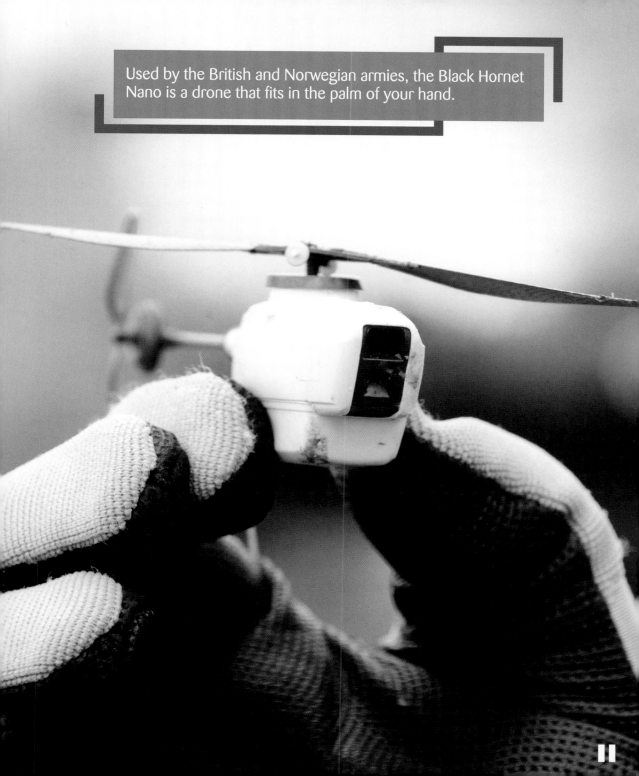

Used by the British and Norwegian armies, the Black Hornet Nano is a drone that fits in the palm of your hand.

THRUST AND LIFT

Like all aircraft, drones need to generate thrust and lift in order to fly. Many military drones have **propellers** or jet engines. Recreational and commercial drones, on the other hand, are rotorcraft. Like helicopters, their rapidly spinning blades create the lift needed to get them off the ground.

Drones have flight controllers, which you can think of as computerized "brains" that help them during flight. They also have built-in GPS and other equipment that help them adjust their path while in flight. They have sensors that prevent them from flying into objects, too. Digital cameras are a common addition to many drones. If a drone is expected to carry a **payload**, then clamps or some other device is needed to keep the cargo safe during flight.

THE FOUR FORCES OF FLIGHT

LIFT: An upward force acting on an object.

THRUST: The force that moves an object in a given direction.

WEIGHT: The force of gravity acting upon a body.

DRAG: The force that acts on a body in the opposite direction of the body's movement.

COMMERCIAL DRONE

CAMERA

ROTOR

POWER

CARGO BOX

GRABBERS

All drones require the same basic equipment, such as engines and a power or fuel source. Commercial drones often need clamps or grabbers to hold on to cargo.

HOW DO DRONES WORK?

There are many different ways to launch and control a drone. Some drones, such as the RQ-11 Raven, are light enough to be launched by hand. Many drones, such as the MQ-1 Predator, take off from runways like ordinary aircraft. Other drones become airborne by catapult launchers, which are small and easy to use. Quadcopters and other rotorcraft drones are capable of vertical takeoffs and landings, or VTOL.

STAYING IN THE AIR

People can program their drone to stay at the same height in the air during flight. A sensor inside the drone registers the altitude, and a chip tells the drone to remain at that height.

Some drones are so advanced that they require large control stations, such as the one pictured here.

While some drones have programmable autopilots, many still require a human pilot, or operator. Some drones are flown by remote control, such as model airplanes. You can even fly a drone using a smartphone or tablet. Many drones, especially those used by the military and law enforcement agencies, are controlled through remote computer stations that resemble the cockpit of traditional aircraft.

THE FIRST COMMERCIAL DRONES

You probably don't give much thought to the air above us. To most of us, the sky looks like an open and empty space. But the sky is often full of aircraft, including drones.

There are many rules and **regulations** about what can fly in the air and when it can fly. In the United States, the Federal Aviation Administration, or FAA, is in charge of making sure the skies above us are safe. For that reason, the FAA must approve any drones that are used commercially.

In the summer of 2013, the FAA approved the use of small drones for aerial **surveillance** of the Arctic Ocean. One year later, in June 2014, the FAA approved the use of drones over land for the first time. BP, which is one of the world's largest energy companies, was given approval to use drones to survey pipelines, roads, and equipment at its oil fields in Alaska.

A drone just like this one became the first commercial drone allowed over the United States when the FAA granted BP permission to use it to survey its oil fields in Alaska.

DRONES AND THE FAA

The U.S. military, intelligence agencies, and law enforcement agencies have their own sets of rules and regulations regarding drone operation. Commercial drone use in the United States is regulated by the FAA.

The FAA has proposed a number of strict regulations for commercial drone operation. Operators must be over the age of 17 and pass a test about drone safety and operation. Commercial drones can only be flown during the day. They must not travel faster than 100 miles (161 km) per hour, and they can only fly up to 500 feet (152 m) in the air. Drones must remain in sight of operators, and the operator must be able to take manual control of the drone at any time.

Recently, the FAA has said it's looking into changing its laws about drones, as pilots have reported more drones getting in the way of safe takeoffs and landings. Crowded airspace isn't good for anyone, so it's unlikely you'll see a **fleet** of drones filling the skies anytime soon.

AMAZON AND GOOGLE TAKE TO THE AIR

Once the FAA decided to allow commercial drones to operate over the United States, companies around the country began looking for ways they could use drones. Two of the first companies to enter the commercial drone race were Amazon and Google.

As early as 2013, Amazon **CEO** Jeff Bezos appeared on national television to announce Amazon Prime Air, which is a drone-based delivery system. Amazon drones would be able to deliver packages weighing less than 5 pounds (2.3 kg) within 30 minutes of ordering.

In 2015, Google started developing a solar-powered drone called Project Titan. Project Titan would allow Google to provide Internet service from the air. Like Amazon, Google has also been working on a system of delivery using drones known as Project Wing.

THE DRONE WILL SEE YOU NOW

Google is interested in turning drones into flying ambulances. Medical professionals could provide advice through the drone, which could also deliver first aid kits and other lifesaving supplies.

STEP 1

Place an online order.

STEP 2

Amazon staff packs item into a box.

STEP 4

Drone flies the box directly to the delivery location.

STEP 3

The box is picked up by a drone.

Drones could revolutionize how we shop online. Imagine placing an order on the Internet and having it delivered within 30 minutes—by drone!

SPECIAL DELIVERY

Amazon and Google aren't the only companies interested in using drones for delivery. Delivery drones could allow businesses to ship products to customers without needing to pay a human delivery person. It would allow small businesses to reach more customers, since distance would no longer be a barrier. However, the biggest hurdle in drone delivery is weight. Most drones available for commercial use are small and can't carry heavy loads.

THE WACKY WORLD OF DRONES

People have come up with some crazy uses for drones, from the dry cleaner in Philadelphia that uses a drone to deliver clean clothes, to the man who used a drone to propose to his girlfriend.

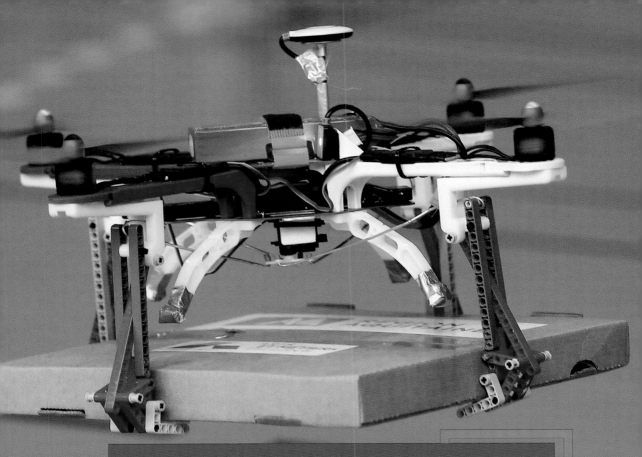

In May 2015, a student in France built this pizza delivery drone. It looks like everyone is ready for food delivery by drone.

Food businesses might benefit the most from drone-based delivery. In 2012, a team of engineers in California created the Burrito Bomber, which is a drone that uses GPS to drop burritos by **parachute**. The following year, Domino's Pizza UK posted a video on the Internet showing the Domicopter, an eight-rotor drone, carrying pizzas over the English countryside.

SAY CHEESE!

Most of the drones you can buy can be equipped with a simple digital camera. It's easy to see why drones are now being used for commercial photography and filming.

Traditionally, news stations have used helicopters to film some of what we see on the news. Helicopters are huge and expensive. Lighter and smaller drones, however, can fly lower and into smaller spaces than aircraft can reach.

In addition to filming, drones can also be used to take aerial photographs. A photographer with a camera-equipped drone could be hired by a real estate agent to take overhead photographs of properties for sale. Photographers have even started using drones to take aerial photographs of weddings.

Photographers may be the first to fully benefit from commercial drone legalization. Most drones used by people can easily carry a digital camera.

IN CASE OF EMERGENCY

Delivery and aerial photography aren't the only uses for commercial drones. Some companies want to use drones for search-and-rescue missions or emergency services.

When a disaster such as a hurricane or building collapse occurs, drones can be sent into the area to survey damage and search for survivors. Food, water, and other supplies can be delivered to people who are trapped. Drones can determine when it's safe to send in human rescue parties. Drones can also be used as aerial lifeguards, locating swimmers in need and delivering life preservers.

Drones could one day be used to deliver medicine and medical supplies to remote or hard-to-reach places. In 2013, German delivery company DHL successfully used a drone to carry a package containing medical supplies from one side of the Rhine River to the other.

This DHL Parcelcopter was designed to stand up to the high winds and bad weather conditions around Germany's North Sea. Here, a test pilot gets ready to put the drone to work.

FLYING OR SPYING?

In addition to safety issues, many people are concerned that drones flying over our cities could create a huge privacy issue. Drones are already used by the military, intelligence agencies, and law enforcement to spy on criminals and terrorists. What would prevent people from using commercial drones to spy on **law-abiding** citizens?

Many federal and local laws prevent recreational and commercial drones from flying near private property and photographing people without permission. However, if companies such as Amazon, Google, or DHL start flying hundreds or thousands of drones over the United States, it would be impossible to keep them all away from private property. Groups such as the Citizens Education Project are trying to get lawmakers to pass firm legislation regarding drone use, data collection, and privacy.

Cameras are one of the most common additions to drones. This has caused many people to raise concerns about privacy and commercial drone use.

THE FUTURE OF COMMERCIAL DRONES

Drones are still a relatively new technology, especially in the hands of civilians. There are certainly many uses for these tiny flying machines, from delivering food to saving lives. Of course, as with any new technology, a number of safety concerns need to be addressed before the skies are filled with drones.

While companies such as Amazon and Google may be ready to launch drones into the skies, the FAA isn't willing to allow widespread drone use without more research. Legalization of commercial drone use could be a huge benefit for the American economy—not just for the companies that use them, but also for the companies that build and improve them.

GLOSSARY

autonomous: Not controlled by others or by outside forces.

CEO: Chief executive officer of a company.

civilian: Not having to do with the military.

fleet: A group of aircraft operating together.

intelligence: Secret information that a government collects about an enemy or a potential enemy.

law-abiding: Following the law.

parachute: A cloth that fills with air and allows a heavy object to lower to the ground slowly when dropped from an aircraft.

payload: The passengers or cargo carried by an aircraft.

propeller: A set of blades that spin quickly to make a plane fly.

regulation: A rule, law, or principle that guides behavior.

rotor: The hub and rotating blade that supply lift for a rotorcraft, such as a helicopter.

surveillance: Continuous observation of a person, place, or group in order to gather information.

technology: The tools people use and the way that they use them.

vehicle: A machine that is powered to move on its own.

INDEX

WEBSITES

Due to the changing nature of Internet links, PowerKids Press has developed an online list of websites related to the subject of this book. This site is updated regularly. Please use this link to access the list: www.powerkidslinks.com/dron/comm